Y0-EFT-702

Westminster Confession of
Faith.

The Westminster confession
of faith

THE WESTMINSTER CONFESSION OF FAITH

A Modern Study Edition

by
John H. Ball, III
and
Philip Rollinson

Summertown Texts
Signal Mountain, Tennessee

Revised ARP Edition
1991
ISBN: 0-9614303-4-63

Copyright ©1979, 1991 The Summertown
Company, Incorporated

Printed in the United States of America by Faith Printing Company.

CONTENTS

PREFACE

The *Standards of the Associate Reformed Presbyterian Church* consist of the following: the Westminster Confession of Faith, the Westminster Larger Catechism, the Westminster Shorter Catechism, the Form of Government, the Book of Discipline, and the Book of Worship.

Over the years, various revisions have been made to the Westminster Confession of Faith. The present document is one that is distinctly Associate Reformed Presbyterian. The modern English version of this document, prepared by Dr. John Ball and Dr. Philip Rollinson for Summertown Texts, has been approved by the General Synod of the Associate Reformed Presbyterian Church for use *as a study tool complementary to, but not in place of,* our Westminster Confession of Faith in its more traditional form as found in our *Standards*.

The Board of Christian Education of the Associate Reformed Presbyterian Church commends this modern English version as an excellent study guide for the purpose indicated above.

September 27, 1990

J. B. Hendrick, Director,

Office of Christian Education
General Synod,
Associate Reformed Presbyterian Church

Chapter 1

Concerning Holy Scripture

1. Our natural understanding and the works of creation and providence so clearly show God's goodness, wisdom, and power that human beings have no excuse for not believing in Him. However, these means alone cannot provide that knowledge of God and of His will which is necessary for salvation. Therefore it pleased the Lord at different times and in various ways to reveal Himself and to declare that this revelation contains His will for His church. Afterwords it pleased God to put this entire revelation into writing so that the truth might be better perserved and transmitted and that the church, confronted with the corruption of the flesh and the evil purposes of Satan and the world, might be more securely established and comforted. Since God no longer reveals Himself to His people in those earlier ways, Holy Scripture is absolutely essential.

2. What we call Holy Scripture or the written word of God now includes all the books of the Old and the New Testament, which are:

The Old Testament

Genesis, Exodus, Leviticus, Numbers, Deuteronomy, Joshua, Judges, Ruth,1 Samuel, 2 Samuel, 1 Kings, 2 Kings, 1 Chronicles, 2 Chronicles, Ezra,Nehemiah, Esther, Job, Psalms, Proverbs, Ecclesiastes, Song of Solomon,Isaiah, Jeremiah, Lamentations, Ezekiel, Daniel, Hosea, Joel, Amos,Obadiah, Jonah, Micah,Nahum, Habakkuk, Zephaniah, Haggai, Zechariah, Malachi

The New Testament

Matthew, Mark, Luke, John, Acts, Romans, 1 Corinthians, 2 Corinthians,Galatians, Ephesians, Philippians, Colossians, 1

Thessalonians, 2 Thessalonians, 1 Timothy, 2 Timothy, Titus, Philemon, Hebrews, James, 1 Peter, 2 Peter, 1 John, 2 John, 3 John, Jude, Revelation.

All of these books are inspired by God and are the rule of faith and life.

3. The books usually called the Apocrypha are not divinely inspired and are not part of the canon of Scripture. They therefore have no authority in the church of God and are not to be valued or used as anything other than human writings.

4. The Bible speaks authoritatively and so deserves to be believed and obeyed. This authority does not depend on the testimony of any man or church but completely on God, its author, Who is Himself truth. The Bible therefore is to be accepted as true, because it is the word of God.

5. We may be influenced by the testimony of the church to value the Bible highly and reverently, and Scripture itself shows in so many ways that it is God's word; for example, in its spiritual subject matter, in the effectiveness of its teaching, the majesty of its style, the agreement of all its parts, its unified aim from beginning to end (to give all glory to God), the full revelation it makes of the only way of man's salvation, its many other incomparably outstanding features, and its complete perfection. However, we are completely persuaded and assured of the infallible truth and divine authority of the Bible only by the inward working of the Holy Spirit, Who testifies by and with the word in our hearts.

6. The whole purpose of God about everything pertaining to His own glory and to man's salvation, faith, and life is either explicitly stated in the Bible or may be deduced as inevitably and logically following from it. Nothing is at any time to be added to the Bible, either from new revelations of the Spirit or from traditions of men. Nevertheless, we do recognize that the inward illumination of the Spirit of God is necessary for a saving understanding of the things which are revealed in the word. We also recognize that some provisions for the worship of God and the government of the church are similar to secular activities and organizations; these are to be directed according to our natural understanding and our Christian discretion and should conform to the general rules of the word, which are always to be observed.

7. The meanings of all the passages in the Bible are not equally obvious, nor is any individual passage equally clear to everyone. However, everything which we have to know, believe, and observe in order to be saved is so clearly presented and revealed somewhere in the Bible that the uneducated as well as the educated can sufficiently understand it by the proper use of the ordinary means of grace.

8. The Old Testament in Hebrew (the native language of the ancient people of God) and the New Testament in Greek (the language most widely known internationally at the time the New Testament was written) were directly inspired by God and have been kept uncontaminated throughout time by His special care and providence. They are therefore authentic and are to be the church's ultimate source of appeal in every religious controversy. The original languages of the Bible, however, are not understood by all of God's people. But all of God's people have a right to and interest in the Bible, and God Himself commands them to read it thoroughly with awe and reverence for Him. Consequently the Bible should be translated into the native language of every people to whom it is introduced. Then the word of God will live fully in everyone; everyone will be able to worship God in an acceptable way; and all believers may have hope through the endurance and the encouragement of the Bible.

9. The infallible standard for the interpretation of the Bible is the Bible itself. And so any question about the true and complete sense of a passage in the Bible (which is a unified whole) can be answered by referring to other passages which speak more plainly.

10. The Holy Spirit speaking in the Bible is the supreme judge of all religious controversies, all decisions of religious councils, all the opinions of ancient writers, all human teachings, and every private opinion. We are to be satisfied with the judgment of Him Who is and can be the only judge.

Chapter 2

Concerning God and the Holy Trinity

1. There is only one living and true God, Who is infinite in being and perfection, a completely pure spirit, invisible, without body, parts, or emotions, unchangeable, immensely vast, eternal, unsearchable, almighty, completely wise, completely holy, completely free, and completely absolute. He works everything according to the purpose of His own unchangeable and completely righteous will for His own glory. He is completely loving, gracious, merciful, and patient. He overflows with goodness and truth. He forgives wickedness, transgression, and sin, and rewards those who diligently seek Him. His judgments are completely just and awesome; He hates all sin and will not acquit the guilty.

2. God has all life, glory, goodness, and blessedness in and of Himself. He alone is all-sufficient in and unto Himself, nor does He need any of His creations or derive any glory from them. Rather, He manifests His own glory in, by, unto, and on them. He is the only source of all being, by Whom, through Whom, and to Whom everything exists. He has completely sovereign dominion over all things and does with, to, or for them whatever He pleases. Everything is revealed and completely open to Him. His knowledge is infinite, infallible, and does not depend on any created being, so that to Him nothing is conditional or uncertain. He is completely holy in all His purposes, works, and commands. To Him is due whatever worship, service, or obedience He is pleased to require from angels, human beings, and all other creatures.

3. In the unity of the Godhead there are three persons, having one substance, power, and eternity: God the Father, God the Son, and God the Holy Spirit. The Father exists. He is not generated and does not come from any source. The Son is eternally

generated from the Father, and the Holy Spirit eternally comes
from the Father and the Son.

Chapter 3

Concerning God's Eternal Decrees

1. From all eternity and by the completely wise and holy purpose of His own will, God has freely and unchangeably ordained whatever happens. This ordainment does not mean, however, that God is the author of sin (He is not), that He represses the will of His created beings, or that He takes away the freedom or contingency of secondary causes. Rather, the will of created beings and the freedom and contingency of secondary causes are established by Him.

2. Although God knows whatever may or can happen under all possible circumstances, He has not ordered anything because He foresaw it in the future as something which would happen under such circumstances.

3. In order to manifest His glory God has ordered that some men and angels be predestined to everlasting life and that others should be foreordained to everlasting death.

4. This predestination and foreordination of angels and men is precise and unchangeable. The number and identity of angels and men in each group is certain, definite, and unalterable.

5. Before the creation of the world, according to His eternal, unchangeable plan and the hidden purpose and good pleasure of His will, God has chosen in Christ those of mankind who are predestined to life and to everlasting glory. He has done this solely out of His own mercy and love and completely to the praise of His wonderful grace. This choice was completely independent of His foresight of how His created beings would be or act. Neither their faith nor good works nor perseverance had any part in influencing His selection.

6. Just as God has determined that the elect shall be glorified, so, too, in the eternal and completely free purpose of His will He has foreordained all the means by which that election is ac-

complished. And so, those who are chosen, having fallen in Adam, are redeemed by Christ. They are effectually called to faith in Christ by His Spirit working in them at the right time, and they are justified, adopted, sanctified, and kept by His power through faith unto salvation. Only the elect, and no others, are redeemed by Christ, effectually called, justified, adopted, sanctified, and saved.

7. According to the hidden purpose of His own will, by which He offers or withholds mercy at His pleasure, and for the glory of His sovereign power over His creatures, it pleased God not to call the rest of mankind and to ordain them to dishonor and wrath for their sin, to the praise of His glorious justice.

8. This important and mysterious doctrine of predestination must be treated with special discretion and care, so that, paying attention to and obeying the will of God revealed in His word, men may be assured that they have been eternally chosen from the certainty of their effectual calling. In this way the doctrine of predestination will elicit not only our praise, reverence, and admiration for God, but also a humble and diligent life, fully supporting everyone who sincerely obeys the gospel.

Chapter 4

Concerning Creation

1. In the beginning it pleased God the Father, Son, and Holy Spirit to create the world out of nothing in order to reveal the glory of His eternal power, wisdom, and goodness. He made everything in the world, visible and invisible, in the space of six days, and it was very good.

2. After God had made all the other creatures, He created man, male and female, with reasoning, immortal souls. He endowed them with knowledge, righteousness, and true holiness in His own image and wrote His law in their hearts. God also gave them the ability to obey His law and the potential to disobey it; i.e., He gave them freedom of their own will, which could change. In addition to this law written in their hearts, they were commanded not to eat from the Tree of the Knowledge of Good and Evil. As long as they obeyed God's law and kept this commandment, they were happy in fellowship with God and had dominion over the other creatures.

Chapter 5

Concerning Providence

1. God, Who created everything, also upholds everything. He directs, regulates, and governs every creature, action, and thing, from the greatest to the least, by His completely wise and holy providence. He does so in accordance with His infallible foreknowledge and the voluntary, unchangeable purpose of His own will, all to the praise of the glory of His wisdom, power, justice, goodness, and mercy.

2. God is the first cause, and in relationship to Him everything happens unchangeably and infallibly. However, by this same providence, He orders things to happen from secondary causes. As a result of these secondary causes, some things must inevitably happen; others may or may not happen depending on the voluntary intentions of the agents involved; and some things do not have to happen but may, depending on other conditions.

3. God uses ordinary means to work out His providence day by day. But, as He pleases, He may work without, beyond, or contrary to these means.

4. God's providence reveals His almighty power, unknowable wisdom, and infinite goodness. His providence extends even to the fall and to all other sins of angels and men. These sins are not simply allowed by God, but are bound, ordered, and governed by Him in the fulness of His wisdom and power so that they fulfill His own holy purposes. However, the sinfulness still belongs to the creature and does not proceed from God, Whose holy righteousness does not and cannot cause or approve sin.

5. In the fulness of His wisdom, righteousness, and grace God often allows His own children to be tempted in various ways and for a time to pursue the corruption of their own hearts. God does this to chastise them for their previous sins and to reveal to them the hidden strength of corruption and deceitfulness in their

hearts, so that they may be humbled. In addition to various other just and holy results, believers are thereby raised to a closer and more constant dependence on God for their support and are also made more alert in detecting and resisting opportunities to sin.

6. It is different for the wicked and the ungodly. As punishment for their previous sins, God, the righteous judge, spiritually blinds and hardens them in their own sinfulness. From them God not only withholds His grace, by which they might have been spiritually enlightened, but sometimes He also withdraws whatever gift of spiritual understanding they already had and deliberately exposes them to the opportunities for sinning which their corrupt nature naturally seeks. He thereby gives them over to their own desires, to the temptations of the world, and to the power of Satan, and so it happens that they harden themselves even under those circumstances which God uses to soften others.

7. Just as the providence of God in general extends to every creature, so, in a very special way it takes care of His church and orders all things for her good.

Chapter 6

Concerning the Fall of Man, Sin, and the Punishment for Sin

1. Our first parents were led astray by the cunning temptation of Satan and sinned in eating the forbidden fruit. It pleased God to allow them to sin, because in His wisdom and holiness He planned to order their sin to His own glory.

2. By this sin they fell from their original righteousness and fellowship with God, and so became dead in sin and completely polluted in all their faculties and parts of body and soul.

3. Since Adam and Eve are the root of all mankind, the guilt for this sin has been imputed to all human beings, who are their natural descendants and have inherited the same death in sin and the same corrupt nature.

4. This original corruption completely disinclines, incapacitates, and turns us away from every good, while it completely inclines us to every evil. From it proceed all actualized sins.

5. During life on earth this corrupt nature remains in those who are regenerated, and, although it is pardoned and deadened in Christ, yet it and all its impulses are truly and properly sinful.

6. Every sin, both original and actual, transgresses the righteous law of God and brings guilt on the sinner. Every sinner is consequently subjected to the wrath of God, the curse of the law, and death, with all the resultant miseries, spiritual, temporal, and eternal.

Chapter 7

Concerning God's Covenant with Man

1. The distance between God and His creation is so great, that, although reasoning creatures owe Him obedience as their creator, they nonetheless could never realize any blessedness or reward from Him without His willingly condescending to them. And so it pleased God to provide for man by means of covenants.

2. The first covenant made with man was a covenant of works. In it life was promised to Adam and through him to his descendants, on the condition of perfect, personal obedience.

3. By his fall, man made himself incapable of life under that covenant, and so the Lord made a second, the covenant of grace. In it He freely offers sinners life and salvation through Jesus Christ. In order to be saved he requires faith in Jesus and promises to give His Holy Spirit to all who are ordained to life so that they may be willing and able to believe.

4. This covenant of grace is frequently identified in Scripture as a testament, in reference to the death of Jesus Christ, the testator, and to the everlasting inheritance and everything included in that legacy.

5. This covenant was administered differently in the time of the law and in the time of the gospel. Under the law it was administered by promises, prophecies, sacrifices, circumcision, the paschal lamb, and other types and ordinances given to the Jewish people, all foreshadowing Christ. For that time the covenant administered under the law through the operation of the Spirit was sufficient and effective in instructing the elect and building up their faith in the promised Messiah, by Whom they had full remission of their sins and eternal salvation. This administration is called the Old Testament.

6. Under the gospel Christ Himself, the substance of God's grace, was revealed. The ordinances of this New Testament are

the preaching of the word and the administration of the sacraments of baptism and the Lord's supper. Although these are fewer in number and are administered with more simplicity and less outward glory, yet they are available to all nations, Jews and Gentiles, and in them the spiritual power of the covenant of grace is more fully developed. There are not then two essentially different covenants of grace, but one and the same covenant under different dispensations.

Chapter 8

Concerning Christ the Mediator

1. In His eternal purpose it pleased God to choose and ordain the Lord Jesus, His only begotten Son, to be the mediator between God and man. Jesus is the prophet, priest, and king, the head and savior of His church, the heir of all things, and judge of the world. From all eternity God gave Him a people to be His seed and to be in time redeemed, called, justified, sanctified, and glorified by Him.

2. The Son of God, the second person of the Trinity, is truly the eternal God, of one substance and equal with the Father. In the fulness of time He took on Himself the nature of man, with all the essential qualities and ordinary frailties of man--except that He was sinless. Jesus was conceived by the power of the Holy Spirit in the womb of the Virgin Mary out of her substance. These two complete, perfect, and distinct natures, the Godhead and the manhood, were inseparably joined together in the one person of Jesus without being altered, disunited, or jumbled. The person Jesus is truly God and truly man, yet one Christ, the only mediator between God and man.

3. His human nature being thus united to the divine, the Lord Jesus was sanctified and anointed with the Holy Spirit beyond all measure. He had in Him all the treasures of wisdom and knowledge, and in Him it pleased the Father that all fulness should dwell. God's purpose was that Jesus, being holy, harmless, undefiled, and full of grace and truth, should be completely equipped to execute the office of mediator and guarantor. Jesus did not take this office on Himself but was called to it by His Father, Who gave and commanded Him to use all power and judgment.

4. The Lord Jesus undertook this office completely voluntarily. In order to discharge it He was made under and perfectly fulfilled

the law. He endured extremely severe torment in His soul and extremely painful suffering in His body. He was crucified and died. He was buried and remained under the power of death, but His body did not decay. On the third day He arose from the dead with the same body in which He suffered and with which He also ascended into heaven. There He sits at the right hand of His Father, interceding for believers. He will return to judge men and angels at the end of the world.

5. By His perfect obedience and sacrifice, offered up to God once and for all through the eternal Spirit, the Lord Jesus has completely satisfied the justice of His Father and purchased not only reconciliation but also an everlasting inheritance in the kingdom of heaven for everyone whom the Father has given to Him.

6. Although the work of redemption was not actually done by Christ until after His incarnation, yet the power, effectiveness, and benefits of it were given to the elect in all ages from the beginning of the world by means of those promises, types, and sacrifices which revealed Him and indicated that He would be the seed of the woman, would bruise the serpent's head, and was the lamb slain from the beginning of the world. Jesus Christ is yesterday and today and forever the same.

7. In the work of mediation Christ acts according to both His natures, each nature doing what is proper to each. However, because of the unity of His person, Scripture sometimes attributes what is proper to one nature to the person indicated by the other nature.

8. Christ insures with absolute certainty that everyone for whom He purchased redemption actually accepts and receives it. He makes intercession for them, reveals the mysteries of salvation to them in and by the word, and effectively persuades them to believe and obey by His Spirit. He governs their hearts by His word and Spirit and overcomes all their enemies by His almighty power and wisdom in such ways as are most in agreement with His wonderful and unknowable administration of things.

Chapter 9

Concerning Free Will

1. God has given man a will, which by nature is free, i.e., it is not forced or necessarily inclined toward good or evil.

2. In his state of innocence man had complete freedom and the natural ability to will and to do what is good and pleasing to God. God also made man so that he could lose that freedom.

3. Man fell into a state of sin by his disobedience and so completely lost his ability to will any spiritual good involving salvation. Consequently fallen man is by nature completely opposed to spiritual good, is dead in sin, and is unable by his own strength either to convert himself or to prepare himself for conversion.

4. When God converts a sinner and brings him into a state of grace, He frees him from his natural enslavement to sin. By God's grace alone, freely given, sinful man is enabled to will and to do what is spiritually good. However, since the old sinful nature also remains, the believer cannot consistently or perfectly will to do what is good but also wills evil.

5. The will of man is perfectly free and permanently inclined to do good alone only in the state of glory.

Chapter 10

Concerning Effectual Calling

1. At the right time, appointed by Him, God effectually calls all those and only those whom He has predestined to life. He calls them by His word and Spirit out of their natural state of sin and death into grace and salvation through Jesus Christ. He enlightens their minds spiritually with a saving understanding of the things of God. He takes away their heart of stone and gives them a heart of flesh. He renews their wills and by His almighty power leads them to what is good. And so He effectually draws them to Jesus Christ. But they come to Jesus voluntarily, having been made willing by God's grace.

2. This effectual call is freely made by God and is entirely an act of His special grace. It does not depend on anything God foresaw about the person called, who is completely passive. God Himself gives life and renewal by the Holy Spirit. He thereby enables each person to answer His call and to accept the grace He offers and actually gives.

3. Elect infants, dying in infancy, are regenerated and saved by Christ through the Spirit, Who works when, where, and how He pleases. The same is true of all other elect persons who are incpable of being outwardly called by the ministry of the word.

4. Others, not elect, may be called by the ministry of the word, and the Spirit may work in them in some of the same ways He works in the elect. However, they never truly come to Christ and therefore cannot be saved. And, of course, people, not professing the Christian religion, cannot be saved in any other way at all, no matter how hard they try to live a moral life according to their own understanding or try to follow the rules of some other religion. To say they can be saved is extremely harmful and should be abhorred.

Chapter 11

Concerning Justification

1. Those whom God effectually calls He also freely justifies. He does not pour righteousness into them but pardons their sins and looks on them and accepts them as if they were righteous--not because of anything worked in them or done by them, but for Christ's sake alone. He does not consider their faith itself, the act of believing, as their righteousness or any other obedient response to the gospel on their part. Rather He imputes to them the obedience and judicial satisfaction earned by Christ. For their part, they receive and rest on Christ and His righteousness by faith (and this faith is not their own but is itself a gift of God).

2. Faith, thus receiving and resting on Christ and His righteousness, is the only means of justification. In the person justified, however, it is always accompanied by all the other saving graces and is not a dead faith, but works by love.

3. By His obedience and death Christ completely discharged the debt of all those who are so justified, and He made the correct, real, and full satisfaction to His Father's justice on their behalf. Since Christ was voluntarily given by the Father for them, and since His obedience and satisfaction were accepted in their place and not for anything in them, their justification is the result only of His free grace--so that both the perfect justice and the rich grace of God might be glorified in the justification of sinners.

4. From all eternity God decreed the justification of all the elect, and in the fulness of time Christ died for their sins and rose again for their justification. Nevertheless, the elect are not justified until the Holy Spirit in due time does actually apply Christ to them.

5. God continues to forgive the sins of those who are justified. Although they can never fall from the state of justification, they may by their sins come under God's fatherly displeasure and not have a sense of His presence with them until they humble them-

selves, confess their sins, ask for forgiveness, and renew their faith in repentance.

6. The justification of believers under the Old Testament was in all these respects identical with the justification of believers under the New Testament.

Chapter 12

Concerning Adoption

1. God guarantees the gift of adoption for all those who are justified in and for the sake of His only son, Jesus Christ. Those adopted enjoy the liberties and privileges of God's children, have His name put on them, receive the Spirit of adoption, have access to the throne of grace with boldness, and are enabled to cry, Abba, Father. They are pitied, protected, provided for, and disciplined by Him as a father. They are never cast off, however, and are sealed until the day of redemption and inherit the promises as heirs of everlasting salvation.

Chapter 13

Concerning Sanctification

1. Those who are effectually called and regenerated have a new heart and a new spirit created in them. They are additionally sanctified, actually and personally, by the power of Christ's death and resurrection and by His word and Spirit dwelling in them. The power of sin ruling over the whole body is destroyed, and the desires of the old self are more and more weakened and killed. At the same time the ability to practice true holiness, without which no one will see the Lord, is brought to life and strengthened by all the saving graces.

2. This sanctification works in the whole person, but not completely or perfectly in this life. The old sinful nature retains some of its control in body, mind, and spirit. And so a continual and irreconcilable war goes on in every believer. The old nature tries to get its way in opposition to the Spirit, and the Spirit fights to assert authority over the flesh.

3. Although the old nature temporarily wins battles in this warfare, the continual strengthening of the sanctifying Spirit of Christ enables the regenerate nature in each believer to overcome. And so the saints grow in grace, perfecting holiness in the fear of God.

Chapter 14

Concerning Saving Faith

1. The gift of faith makes it possible for the souls of the elect to be saved by believing in Jesus Christ. This gift is the work of the Spirit of Christ in the hearts of the elect and is ordinarily accomplished by the ministry of the word. It is also increased and strengthened by the word, by prayer, and by the administration of the sacraments.

2. By this faith a Christian believes whatever is revealed in the word to be the true, authentic, authoritative statement of God Himself. By this faith the believer also acts according to what particular passages in the word say. By faith the believer humbly submits to and obeys God's various commands. He trembles at God's awesome threats and eagerly embraces His promises about this life and the life to come. But the chief actions of saving faith are accepting, receiving, and resting on Christ alone for justification, sanctification, and eternal life, in the power of the covenant of grace.

3. This faith has different degrees of strength and weakness. It may be attacked and weakened often and in many ways, but it gets the victory. In many believers it matures and becomes completely assured through Christ, Who both creates and perfects our faith.

Chapter 15

Concerning Repentance Leading to Life

1. Repentance which leads to life is the blessed product of the gospel working in believers' lives. Along with the doctrine of faith in Christ it is a doctrine to be preached by every minister of the gospel.

2. In this repentance the sinner is able to see his sins as God sees them, as filthy and hateful, and as involving great danger to the sinner, because they are completely contrary to the holy nature and righteous law of God. Understanding that God in Christ is merciful to those who repent, the sinner suffers deep sorrow for and hates his sins, and so he determines to turn away from all of them. And turning to God, he tries to walk with Him according to all His commandments.

3. Although repentance is not any satisfaction for sin and does not cause the forgiveness of sins (since forgiveness is an act of God's voluntary grace in Christ), yet it is necessary to all sinners, and no one may expect to be forgiven without it.

4. Just as there is no sin so small that it does not deserve damnation, so there is no sin so great that it can bring damnation upon those who truly repent.

5. Believers should not be satisfied with general repentance. Rather it is everyone's duty to try to repent of every individual sin individually.

6. Everyone is also bound to confess privately his sins to God and to pray for forgiveness for them. Confession, prayer for forgiveness, and the forsaking of sins which have been forgiven will find God's mercy. Similarly, anyone who sins against his spiritual brother or the church should be willing to confess, privately or publicly, to demonstrate sorrow for his sin, and openly to state his repentance to those whom he has hurt. They in turn are to be reconciled to him and to receive him in love.

Chapter 16

Concerning Good Works

1. Good works are only those works identified as good by God and commanded by Him in His holy word. They do not include other works, no matter how well-intentioned in design or zealously promoted by men.

2. These good works, done in obedience to God's commandments, are the fruit and evidence of a true and living faith. By them believers show their thankfulness, strengthen their assurance of salvation, edify their brothers in the Lord, and become ornaments of all those who profess the gospel. Good works in believers silence the criticism of the enemies of the gospel. They also glorify God by showing that believers are the workmanship and creation of Jesus Christ, because their aim is that holiness of living which leads to eternal life.

3. Believers get the ability to do good works entirely from the Spirit of Christ. In addition to the other particular effects of God's grace already received, believers must be directed by the Holy Spirit in order to will and to do what pleases God. However, they are not therefore to grow spiritually lazy, waiting for some special guidance from the Spirit before doing anything commanded by God. Rather, they should diligently attempt to identify what good works God has commanded in His word and then try their best to do all of them, praying earnestly and daily for the empowering and enabling of the Holy Spirit, Who lives in them.

4. Those believers who do the best that can be done in obeying God in this life can never do more or even as much as He requires. Indeed they fall short of much which they are bound to do.

5. We cannot, of course, by our best works deserve to be forgiven for our sins and to receive eternal life from God. There is that great disproportion between our best works in this life and the glory which is going to be revealed in us, and there is the infinite

distance between us and God, Who does not profit from our best works and is not satisfied by them for the debt of our previous sins. When we have done all we can, we have only done our duty and are unprofitable servants. Since the goodness of our best works in fact proceeds from His Spirit and since, insofar as they are done by us, our best works are defiled and mixed with our weakness and imperfection, they cannot therefore even stand the scrutiny of God's judgment.

6. Nevertheless, since the persons of believers are accepted through Christ, their good works in this life are also accepted in Him. It is not as though they were perfect in God's sight but that God, looking on them in His Son, is pleased to accept and reward what is sincerely done, even though accompanied by much weakness and imperfection.

7. Works done by people who have not been spiritually reborn may be the same as those commanded by God and may be of good use to them and to others. However, since they do not proceed from a heart purified by faith, are not done in the right way, i.e., in response to God's word, and are not done for the right purpose, the glory of God, they are therefore sinful and cannot please God or make a person fit to receive grace from God. Nevertheless, it is more sinful and displeasing to God not to do such works than to do them.

Chapter 17

Concerning the Perseverance of the Saints

1. Those whom God has accepted in His Son and has effectually called and sanctified by His Spirit can never completely or finally fall out of their state of grace. Rather, they shall definitely continue in that state to the end and are eternally saved.

2. This endurance of the saints does not depend on their own free will but on God's unchangeable decree of election, flowing from his voluntary, unchangeable love. It also depends on the effectiveness of the merit and intercession of Jesus Christ, on the indwelling Spirit and indwelling seed of God in the saints, and on the nature of the covenant of grace. All these establish the certainty and infallibility of their preservation.

3. Nevertheless, the temptations of Satan, the world, and their old carnal nature, along with neglect of the means of their preservation, may lead believers to commit serious sins and to continue in them for a time. They consequently displease God and grieve His Holy Spirit, have some of the fruit of God's grace and His comforts taken away from them, have their hearts hardened and their consciences wounded, hurt and offend others, and bring temporal judgments on themselves.

Chapter 18

Concerning the Assurance of Grace and Salvation

1. Hypocrites and other unregenerate men may deceive themselves with false hopes and carnal presumptions about their being in God's favor and about their being saved. Their presumptions will die with them. However, those who truly believe in the Lord Jesus, who honestly love Him and try to walk in good conscience before Him, may in this life be assured with certainty that they are in a state of grace. They may also rejoice in the hope of the glory of God, and they will never be ashamed of that hope.

2. This certainty is not based on the fallible hope of guesswork or probabilities. Rather, it is the infallible assurance of faith, established on the divine truth of the promises of salvation. There is also the inner evidence of spiritual insight, given to us by God, to which these promises are directed. And there is the testimony of the Spirit of adoption, witnessing with our spirits that we are the children of God. This Spirit is the pledge of our inheritance. By Him we are sealed until the day of redemption.

3. This infallible assurance is not so essential to faith that a true believer may not have doubts and conflicts about it, possibly wait some time for it, and grow into it. But since the Spirit enables believers to know the things which are freely given to them by God, every believer may come to a full assurance of salvation by the ordinary working of the Spirit without unusual revelation. Therefore it is every believer's duty to establish the certainty of his calling and election so that his heart may be filled with peace and joy in the Holy Spirit, with love and thankfulness to God, and with strength and cheerfulness of obedience. These are the true products of assurance, which is never conducive to an undisciplined life.

4. The assurance true believers have of their salvation may be shaken, lessened, or interrupted for various reasons: from neglecting to preserve it; from committing some particular sin, which wounds the conscience and grieves the Spirit; from some sudden or strong temptation; or from God's withdrawing the sense of His presence and allowing them to walk in darkness. Nevertheless, they are never completely without God's seed, the life of faith, the love of Christ and of other believers, and the sincere heart and obedient conscience, out of which the Spirit may revive this assurance in due time and by which they are in the meantime kept from complete despair.

Chapter 19

Concerning the Law of God

1. God gave Adam a law as a covenant of works. He required Adam and all his descendants to obey this law, individually, completely, perpetually, and in precise accordance with its provisions. God promised life for keeping it and threatened death for disobeying it, and He gave man the power and ability to keep it.

2. After the fall this law continued to be a perfect rule of righteousness and was given, as such, by God on Mount Sinai in the ten commandments, written on two tablets. The first four commandments establish our obligations to God and the remaining six our obligations to human beings.

3. In addition to this law, ordinarily called the moral law, it pleased God to give the people of Israel, as a pre-Christian assembly of believers, ceremonial laws, containing many typical ordinances. Some of these ordinances pertain to worship and foreshadow Christ, His grace, actions, suffering, and the benefits to be had from believing in Him. The rest of these ordinances contain various instructions about moral duties. All of these ceremonial laws are now nullified under the New Testament.

4. God also gave the Israelites, as a political body, various judicial laws. These expired with the state of Israel and make no further obligation on God's people than seems appropriate in contemporary legal codes.

5. The moral law, however, does pertain to everyone, saved and unsaved, forever, not just with respect to its content but also in relationship to the authority of God, the Creator, Who gave it. In the gospel Christ does not in any way remove this obligation, but rather strengthens it.

6. Although true believers are not justified or condemned by the law as a covenant of works, the law is nevertheless very useful

to them and to others. As a rule of life, it informs them of God's will and of their obligation to obey it. It also reveals to them the sinful pollution of their nature, hearts, and lives, so that, examining themselves from its point of view, they may become more convinced of the presence of sin in them, more humiliated on account of that sin, and hate sin the more. Thus they gain a better awareness of their need for Christ and for the perfection of His obedience. The prohibitions against sin in the law are also useful in restraining believers from pursuing the desires of their old nature, and the punishments for disobedience in the law show them what their sins deserve and what afflictions they may expect for them in this life, even though they have been freed from the curse threatened in the law. The promises of the law similarly show them that God approves obedience and that blessings may be expected for obedience, although not as their due from the law as a covenant of works. The fact that the law encourages doing good and discourages doing evil does not mean that a person who does good and refrains from evil is under the law and not under grace.

7. None of these uses of the law are contrary to the grace of the gospel. They rather beautifully comply with it, because the Spirit of Christ subdues and enables the will of man to do voluntarily and cheerfully what the will of God, revealed in the law, requires to be done.

Chapter 20

Concerning Christian Freedom and Freedom of Conscience

1. Christ has purchased for believers under the gospel freedom from the guilt of sin, from the the condemning wrath of God, and from the curse of the moral law. He has also freed them from the evil world we live in, from enslavement to Satan, from the dominion of sin, the evil of afflictions, the sting of death, the victory of the grave, and from everlasting damnation. In Christ believers have free access to God and can obey Him, not out of slavish fear, but with a childlike love and a willing mind. All these freedoms were also held by believers under the law. However, under the New Testament, the liberty of Christians has been enlarged to include freedom from the yoke of the ceremonial law, to which the Jewish church was subjected. Christians also have greater boldness of access to the throne of grace and a fuller gift of the Spirit of God than believers ordinarily had under the law.

2. God alone is Lord of the conscience and has left it free from the doctrines and commandments of men which are in any way contrary to or different from His word in matters of faith or worship. And so, believing any such teachings or obeying any such commandments of men for conscience's sake actually betrays true freedom of conscience. Requiring implicit or absolute, blind obedience also destroys freedom of conscience as well as the free use of reason.

3. Those who practice any sin or nourish any sinful desire on the pretext of Christian freedom destroy the whole purpose of Christian freedom, which is that, having been rescued out of the hands of our enemies, we might serve the Lord without fear and in holiness and righteousness before Him all the days of our lives.

4. God intends that the authorities He has ordained on earth and the freedom Christ has purchased should not destroy but mutually uphold and preserve each other. And so, those who oppose any lawful power or the lawful exercise of power, whether civil or ecclesiastical, on the pretext of Christian freedom are actually resisting God. The support, promotion, or practice of such opposition, which contradicts natural understanding or the known principles of Christianity on matters of faith, worship, associations, or the order Christ has established in His church, may lawfully be called to account and proceeded against by the church. The civil authorities may also proceed against such opposition insofar as its character or the way it is promoted and maintained destroys the peace of the church or of society in general.

Chapter 21

Concerning Religious Worship and the Sabbath Day

1. Natural understanding reveals that there is a God, Who is Lord and sovereign over everything, Who is good and does good to everyone, and Who is therefore to be held in awe, loved, praised, called upon, trusted in, and served with all our heart, soul, and might. The acceptable way of worshiping the true God is established by God Himself. God's revealed will so defines and outlines proper worship that neither the imaginations and devices of men nor the suggestions of Satan are to be followed. God is not to be worshiped under any visible representation or in any other way than that prescribed in Holy Scripture.

2. Religious worship is to be given to God, the Father, Son, and Holy Spirit, and only to Him, not to angels, saints, or any other creature. Since the fall this worship must involve a mediator, and there is no other mediator than Christ alone.

3. Prayer with thanksgiving is one part of religious worship and is required by God from all men. In order for prayer to be accepted, it must be made in the name of Jesus, by the help of His Spirit, according to His will, with understanding, reverence, humility, fervor, faith, love, and perseverance, and, if vocal, in a known tongue.

4. Prayer is to be made for lawful things and for people who are alive or may be born, but not for the dead, nor for those who are known to have committed the sin unto death.

5. The ordinary worship of God includes: the reverent and attentive reading of the Scriptures; the sound preaching and conscientious hearing of the word in obedience to God with understanding and faith; singing of psalms with grace in the heart; and the proper administration and right receiving of the sacra-

ments instituted by Christ. Then there are religious oaths and vows, solemn fasting, and thanksgiving on special occasions. Worship should include these at appropriate times, and they should be performed in a holy and religious manner.

6. Under the gospel neither prayer nor any other part of religious worship is tied to or made more acceptable by being performed in any particular place. God is to be worshiped everywhere in spirit and in truth: in private families daily; privately by individuals daily; and regularly in solemn public gatherings, which are not to be carelessly or willfully neglected or forsaken, since God calls us to join other believers in public worship.

7. It is a law of our natural, earthly life that some appropriate amount of time be set aside for the worship of God. In His word God has similarly commanded all men in every age to keep one day in seven holy unto Him as a sabbath. From the beginning of the world up to the resurrection of Christ this sabbath was the last day of the week. Since the resurrection of Christ it has been changed to the first day of the week, called the Lord's day in Scripture, and is to be continued until the end of the world as the Christian sabbath.

8. The sabbath is kept holy unto the Lord, when men: prepare their hearts for it; arrange for their daily affairs to be taken care of beforehand; rest the whole day from their own works and words, and from thoughts about their worldly activities and recreations; and take up the whole time in public and private worship and in the duties of necessity and mercy.

Chapter 22

Concerning Lawful Oaths and Vows

1. Lawful oaths are part of religious worship. On proper occasions believers may solemnly swear and call God to witness that what they assert or promise is true, and they may ask God to judge them according to the truth or falsehood of what they swear.

2. The name of God is the only name by which men should swear, and that name is to be used with holy awe and reverence. Therefore, to swear vainly or rashly by that glorious and mighty name or to swear at all by any other name is sinful and to be abhorred. Just as in important matters an oath is warranted by the word of God, under the New as well as the Old Testament, so a lawful oath, required by legitimate authority in such matters, ought to be taken.

3. Whoever takes an oath ought to consider fully the importance of such a solemn act, and so he should swear to nothing but what he is completely convinced is true. No one may bind himself by an oath to anything but what is good and just, to what he believes to be true, and to what he is able and determined to perform. It is a sin to refuse to swear an oath about anything good and just, when it is required by lawful authority.

4. An oath is to be taken in the plain, ordinary sense of the words used, without any equivocation or mental reservation. It cannot obligate one to sin; but, once taken about anything not sinful, it must be performed, even to one's own harm, and must not be broken, even if made to heretics or atheists.

5. A vow is similar to an oath promising something and should be made with similar religious care and performed with similar faithfulness.

6. A vow should be made to no one but God. In order to be accepted, it should be made voluntarily in a faithful and conscientious way as thanks for mercy received or as a means of getting

what we want. A vow binds us more strictly to necessary duties or to other things to such an extent and for as long as is appropriate.

7. No one may vow to do anything forbidden in the word of God, anything hindering a duty commanded in the word, or anything not in his power, which he has neither the ability nor warrant from God to perform. In this respect Roman Catholic monastic vows of perpetual celibacy, professed poverty, and consistent obedience do not perfect us but are actually superstitious, sinful traps, in which no Christian should entangle himself.

Chapter 23

Concerning Civil Authorities

1. God, the supreme Lord and King of the whole world, has ordained civil authorities to be over people under Him for His own glory and the public good. For this purpose He has armed civil authorities with the power of the sword to defend and encourage those who are good and to punish wrongdoers.

2. It is lawful for Christians to accept and execute offices of civil authority, when that is their calling. In the administration of such offices they should take care to support true religion, justice, and peace, according to the beneficial laws of each government, and in so doing they may lawfully under the New Testament wage war on just and necessary occasions.

3. Civil authorities may not take on themselves the ministering of God's word and the sacraments, the administration of spiritual power, or any interference with matters of faith. But, since the Bible lays unavoidable obligations on all classes of people, civil authorities should execute their duties in submission to God's revealed truth. Government should be administered on Christian principles. Authorities should rule in the fear of God and in accordance with the directions in His word, because they will have to give an account to the Lord Jesus, Whom God has appointed to judge the world. Therefore, civil authorities in Christian countries must promote Christianity as being in the best interests of the people. However, this is to be done in ways which do not violate civil rights, which do not suggest interference in the affairs of the church (the free and independent Kingdom of the Redeemer), and which do not assume any control over people's conscience.

4. It is people's duty to pray for those in authority, to honor them, to pay them taxes and whatever is owed them, to obey their lawful commands, and to be subject to them for conscience's sake.

Unbelief or different religious views on the part of civil authorities does not mean that they are to be disobeyed by believers, including clergymen, in the legitimate pursuit of their duties. The pope, of course, has no power or jurisdiction over civil authorities or the people under them in secular affairs. The pope never has any right to usurp secular authority, particularly capital punishment in cases of what is judged to be heresy or any other fault.

Chapter 24

Concerning Marriage and Divorce

1. Marriage is to be between one man and one woman. It is not lawful for any man to have more than one wife nor for any woman to have more than one husband at the same time.

2. Marriage was ordained: for the mutual help of husband and wife; for the legitimate propagation of mankind; for raising up a holy seed to the church; and for the prevention of moral impurity.

3. All people who are mentally, emotionally, and physically capable may legally marry. But it is the duty of Christians to marry only in the Lord. Therefore, those who profess the true reformed religion should not marry with infidels or other idolaters. The godly should not be unequally yoked in marriage with any who live a notoriously wicked life or who maintain damnable heresies.

4. Marriage should not occur where the nearness of blood relationship is forbidden in the Bible. Incestuous marriage can never be legitimized by any human law or consent of the parties involved. A man may not marry any of his [deceased] wife's relatives who are more closely related to her than he might of his own relatives. The same is true of a woman marrying one of her [deceased] husband's relatives.

5. If adultery or fornication is discovered after a contractual commitment to marry has been made but before the marriage itself, the innocent party has the right to dissolve the contract. In the case of adultery after marriage, it is lawful for the innocent party to sue for divorce and after the divorce to marry someone else, as if the guilty party were dead.

6. Although the corrupt nature of man is inclined to support arguments for the wrong separation of those whom God has joined together in marriage, yet the only causes which warrant dissolving the bond of marriage are adultery or deliberate desertion which cannot be remedied in any way by the church or civil

authority. Proceedings for divorce must be public and orderly, and the persons involved must not be allowed to manage their cases according to their own desires and judgments.

Chapter 25

Concerning the Church

1. The catholic or universal church is invisible and consists of all the elect who have been, are, or ever will be gathered into one under Christ, the head. The church is His body and spouse, the fulness of God, Who fills all in all.

2. The visible church is also catholic or universal under the gospel, i.e., it is not confined to one nation as previously under the Mosaic Law. It consists of everyone in the world who professes the true religion together with their children. The visible church is the kingdom of the Lord Jesus Christ and the house and family of God, outside of which people cannot ordinarily be saved.

3. In order to gather and perfect the saints in this life until the end of the world, Christ has given the ministry, Scriptures, and ordinances of God to this universal, visible church, and by His own presence and Spirit He enables the church to function in this way according to His promise.

4. This universal church has been sometimes more and sometimes less visible. Particular churches, which are members of it, are also more or less pure, depending on how the gospel is accepted and taught, how the ordinances of God are administered, and how public worship is performed.

5. The purest churches under heaven are subject both to impurity and error. Some churches have so degenerated that they are not churches of Christ but synagogues of Satan. Nevertheless, there will always be a church on earth to worship God according to His will.

6. There is no other head of the church than the Lord Jesus Christ. No mere man can in any sense be the head of the church.

Chapter 26

Concerning the Fellowship of the Saints

1. All believers are united to Jesus Christ, their head, by His Spirit and by faith and have fellowship with Him in His grace, suffering, death, resurrection, and glory. United to one another in love, the saints have fellowship in each other's gifts and grace and are obliged to perform those public and private duties which nourish their mutual good, both spiritually and physically.

2. By their profession of faith saints are bound to maintain a holy fellowship and communion with each other in the worship of God and in the performance of other spiritual services for their mutual improvement. They are also bound to help each other in material things according to their different abilities and needs. This fellowship is to be offered, as God gives the opportunities, to everyone in every place who calls on the name of the Lord Jesus.

3. This communion which the saints have with Christ in no way means that they share in His Godhead or are equal with Him in any respect--to affirm either is impious and blasphemous. Neither does their communion with each other take away or infringe the right each person has to own and possess goods and property.

Chapter 27

Concerning the Sacraments

1. Sacraments are holy signs and seals of the covenant of grace. They were instituted by God along with that covenant to represent Christ and His benefits, to confirm our position with and in Him, to demonstrate a visible difference between those who belong to the church and the rest of the world, and solemnly to engage believers in the service of God in Christ according to His word.

2. In every sacrament there is a spiritual relationship or sacramental union between the sign and the thing signified. And so the names and effects of the one are attributed to the other.

3. The grace embodied in or by sacraments in their right use does not come from any power in them. Neither does the effectiveness of a sacrament depend on the devoutness or the intention of whoever administers it. Rather the power and effectiveness of the sacraments are the result of the work of the Spirit and rest on God's word instituting them, since His word authorizes their use and promises benefits to worthy receivers of them.

4. There are only two sacraments ordained by Christ our Lord in the gospel: baptism and the Lord's supper. Neither of these may be administered by anyone but a lawfully ordained minister of the word.

5. The sacraments of the Old Testament signify and reveal in substance the same spiritual things as those of the New.

Chapter 28

Concerning Baptism

1. Baptism is a sacrament of the New Testament, ordained by Jesus Christ. By baptism a person is solemnly admitted into the visible church. Baptism is also a sign and seal of the covenant of grace, of ingrafting into Christ, of rebirth, of remission of sins, and of yielding to God through Jesus Christ to walk in newness of life. By Christ's own direction this sacrament is to be continued in His church until the end of the world.

2. The physical substance to be used in this sacrament is water. The person is to be baptized in the name of the Father, the Son, and the Holy Spirit by a lawfully called minister of the gospel.

3. Dipping the person into the water is not necessary. Baptism is correctly administered by pouring or sprinkling water on the person.

4. Not only those who actually profess faith in and obedience to Christ are to be baptized but also the infants of one or both believing parents.

5. Although it is a great sin to condemn or neglect this sacrament, baptism is not inseparably connected with God's grace and salvation. One can be saved and reborn without baptism, and, on the other hand, everyone who is baptized is not therefore unquestionably reborn.

6. The effectiveness of baptism is not tied to that moment in time in which it is administered. However, by the correct use of this sacrament, the grace promised in it is not only offered but actually embodied and conferred by the Holy Spirit to everyone (adult or infant) to whom that grace is given, according to the purpose of God's own will and in His appointed time.

7. The sacrament of baptism should be administered only once to a person.

Chapter 29

Concerning the Lord's Supper

1. The night Jesus was betrayed He instituted the sacrament of His body and blood, called the Lord's supper, to be observed in His church until the end of the world as a perpetual remembrance of His sacrifice in death and as the seal of all the benefits of that sacrifice for true believers. It also signifies the spiritual nourishment and growth of believers in Jesus and their additional commitment to perform all the duties they owe Him. Finally it is a bond and pledge of believers' communion with Jesus and with each other as members of His mystical body.

2. In this sacrament Christ is not offered up to His Father, nor is any actual sacrifice made for the remission of sins of the living or the dead. Rather this sacrament commemorates Christ's offering up of Himself, by Himself, on the cross once for all, and it spiritually offers up to God every possible praise for that sacrifice. Consequently the so-called sacrifice of the Roman Catholic mass does detestable injustice to Christ's one sacrifice, which is the only propitiation for all the sins of the elect.

3. In the administration of the Lord's supper, Jesus has directed His ministers to declare to the congregation His words instituting this sacrament, to pray, and to bless the bread and wine, which are thus set apart from their ordinary use and put to holy use. His ministers are to take and break the bread, to take the cup, and (communicating themselves, too) to give both to the communicants--but not to anyone else not present at that time in the congregation.

4. Practices contrary to the nature of this sacrament and to the institution of it by Christ are: private masses or receiving the sacrament alone from a priest or anyone else; denying the cup to the congregation; and worshiping the bread and wine themselves

by lifting them up or carrying them around for adoration or reserving them for any counterfeit religious use.

5. The bread and wine in this sacrament, properly set apart to the uses ordained by Christ, so relate to Him crucified that truly and yet only sacramentally they are sometimes called by the name of what they represent, that is, the body and blood of Christ. Even so, they still remain in substance and nature only bread and wine, as they were before their sacramental use.

6. The teaching that the substance of the bread and wine is changed into the substance of Christ's body and blood (usually called transubstantiation) by the consecration of a priest or any other means is objectionable not only to Scripture but even to common sense and reason. Such teaching overturns the nature of the sacrament and has been and is the cause of much superstition and indeed flagrant idolatry.

7. Worthy receivers, physically partaking of the visible substances of this sacrament, do then also by faith actually and in fact, but not physically or bodily, spiritually receive and feed on Christ crucified and on all the benefits of His death. The body and blood of Christ are not then bodily or physically in, with, or under the bread and wine; but they are actually spiritually present to the faith of believers in the administration of this sacrament, just as the bread and wine are physically present.

8. Although ignorant or wicked men may partake of the physical substances in this sacrament, they do not receive what is signified by them. However, by their unworthy coming to the Lord's table they are guilty of His body and blood and damn themselves. Therefore, just as the ignorant and ungodly are not fit to enjoy communion with Christ, neither are they worthy to come to the Lord's table, and, as long as they remain ignorant and ungodly, they cannot and must not be allowed to partake of the holy mystery of communion without committing a great sin against Christ.

Chapter 30

Concerning Condemnation by the Church

1. As king and head of His church, the Lord Jesus has directed the establishment of church government, separate from civil authority, which is to be administered by officers of the church.

2. To these officers are committed the keys of the kingdom of heaven, which empower them: to free people from the guilt of sin or to bind them to it; to close the kingdom of heaven to the unrepentant by the word and condemnation; and to open the kingdom to repentant sinners by the ministry of the gospel and by withdrawing condemnation as the occasion demands.

3. Condemnation by the church is necessary in order to reclaim and regain spiritual brothers who have committed some serious offense; to deter others from committing similar offenses; to purge that leaven which might contaminate the whole lump; to vindicate the honor of Christ and the holy profession of the gospel; and to avoid the wrath of God, which might justly fall on the church, should it allow His covenant and the sacraments to be profaned by notorious and obstinate offenders.

4. The best way to accomplish these purposes is for the officers of the church to act in accordance with the severity of the offense and the guilt of the offender by: (1) warning the offender; (2) excluding him from the sacrament of the Lord's Supper for a time; or (3) excommunicating him from the church.

Chapter 31

Concerning Synods and Councils

1. The assemblies which are generally called synods or councils ought to be held for the better government and continuing improvement of the church.

2. By virtue of their office, ministers themselves, or together with other leaders delegated from particular churches, have the exclusive right to call, adjourn, or dissolve such synods and councils. On rare occasions, civil authorities may properly wish to consult with and seek advice from a synod of ministers and other leaders about religious matters. On such occasions churches ought to cooperate with the authorities.

3. As far as the ministry is concerned, it is the responsibility of synods and councils: to settle controversies of faith and cases relating to matters of conscience; to set down rules and directions for the better administration of the public worship of God and of church government; and to hear complaints in cases of maladministration and authoritatively to settle them. If these decisions conform to the word of God, they are to be accepted reverently and submissively, not only because they agree with the word but also because they rest on authority ordained and arranged by God in His word.

4. Since apostolic times all synods and councils, whether general or local, may make mistakes, and many have. Consequently synods and councils are not to be made a final authority in questions of faith and living but are to be used as an aid to both.

5. Synods and councils should consider and settle only ecclesiastical questions. They are not to meddle in civil affairs which concern the state except in extraordinary cases of modest petitions or in an advisory capacity prompted by religious conscience, when requested by civil authorities.

Chapter 32

Concerning the Condition of Man after Death and the Resurrection of the Dead

1. After death the bodies of human beings decompose and return to dust, but their souls, which do not die or sleep, have an immortal existence and immediately return to God Who created them. The souls of the righteous are then perfected in holiness and are received into the highest heavens, where they behold the face of God in light and glory and wait for the full redemption of their bodies. The souls of the wicked are thrown into hell, where they remain in torment and complete darkness, set apart for the great day of judgment. Scripture recognizes only these two places, and no other, for souls separated from their bodies.

2. Those who are alive at the last day will not die but will be changed. At that time all the dead will be raised with the very same bodies and no other than the same bodies they had before, although with different characteristics, which will be united again to their souls forever.

3. By the power of Christ the bodies of the unjust shall be raised to dishonor, but by His spirit the bodies of the just will be raised to honor and be made according to the pattern of His own glorious body.

Chapter 33

Concerning the Last Judgment

1. God the Father has ordained a day in which He will judge the world in righteousness by Jesus Christ, to Whom He has given all power and judgment. In that day not only will the apostate angels be judged, but all the people who have lived on earth will appear before the court of Christ to give an account of their thoughts, words, and actions, and be judged according to what they have done in the body, whether good or evil.

2. God's purpose in arranging for this day is to show forth the glory of His mercy in the eternal salvation of the elect and the glory of His justice in the damnation of the reprobate, who are wicked and disobedient. At that time the righteous will go into everlasting life and receive that fulness of joy and refreshment which will come from the presence of the Lord. But the wicked, who do not know God and do not obey the gospel of Jesus Christ, will be thrown into eternal torment and punished with everlasting destruction away from the presence of the Lord and the glory of His power.

3. Christ wants us to be completely convinced that there is going to be a day of judgment, as a deterrent to sin for everyone and as an added consolation for the godly in their suffering. He has also made sure that no one knows when that day will be, so that we may never rest secure in our worldly surroundings, but, not knowing what hour the Lord will come, we must always be alert and may always be ready to say, "Come, Lord Jesus, come quickly." Amen.

Chapter 34

Concerning the Holy Spirit

1. The Holy Spirit, the third person in the Trinity, proceeding from the Father and the Son, of the same substance and equal in power and glory, is, together with the Father and the Son, to be believed in, loved, obeyed, and worshiped throughout all ages.

2. He is the Lord and Giver of life, everywhere present, and is the source of all good thoughts, pure desires, and holy counsels in men. By Him the prophets were moved to speak the word of God, and all the writers of the Holy Scriptures inspired to record infallibly the mind and will of God. The dispensation of the gospel is especially committed to Him. He prepares the way for it, accompanies it with His persuasive power, and urges its message upon the reason and conscience of men, so that they who reject its merciful offer are not only without excuse but are also guilty of resisting the Holy Spirit.

3. The Holy Spirit, Whom the Father is ever willing to give to all who ask him, is the only efficient agent in the application of redemption. He regenerates men by his grace, convicts them of sin, moves them to repentance, and persuades and enables them to embrace Jesus Christ by faith. He unites all believers to Christ, dwells in them as their Comforter and Sanctifier, gives to them the spirit of Adoption and Prayer, and performs all those gracious offices by which they are sanctified and sealed unto the day of redemption.

4. By the indwelling of the Holy Spirit all believers, being vitally united to Christ, Who is the Head, are thus united one to another in the church, which is His body. He calls and anoints ministers for their holy office, qualifies all other officers in the church for their special work, and imparts various gifts and graces to its members. He gives efficacy to the word and to the ordinances of

the gospel. By Him the church will be preserved, increased, purified, and at last made perfectly holy in the presence of God.

Chapter 35

Concerning the Gospel

1. God in infinite and perfect love, having provided in the covenant of grace, through the mediation and sacrifice of the Lord Jesus Christ, a way of life and salvation, sufficient for and adapted to the whole lost race of man, freely offers this salvation to all men in the gospel.

2. In the gospel God declares His love for the world and His desire that all men should be saved; reveals fully and clearly the only way of salvation; promises eternal life to all who truly repent and believe in Christ; invites and commands all to embrace the offered mercy; and by His Spirit accompanying the word pleads with men to accept His gracious invitation.

3. It is the duty and privelege of everyone who hears the gospel immediately to accept its merciful provisions; and they who continue in impenitence and unbelief incur aggravated guilt and perish by their own fault.

4. Since there is no other way of salvation than that revealed in the gospel, and since in the divinely established and ordinary method of grace faith comes by hearing the word of God, Christ has commissioned his church to go into all the world and to make disciples of all nations. All believers are, therefore, under obligation to sustain the ordinances of the Christian religion where they are already established, and to contribute by their prayers, gifts, and personal efforts to the extension of the kingdom of Christ throughout the whole earth.